BLUE BABE

The Story of a Steppe Bison Mummy From Ice Age Alaska

Mary Lee Guthrie

White Mammoth
Fairbanks, Alaska

A lone bull steppe bison is grazing the bottom of an open slope, above a brushy ravine, in the dusk of an early winter evening. Intent on the next clump of dried grass, his nostrils suddenly fill with an alarming scent. A pair of lions bursts from snowy cover along the creek. There are snorts and thrusts: action impossible to follow in the failing light, followed by the unmistakable sounds of death.

These lions, and perhaps a third, feed on the bison for several days, but as cold soaks through the carcass, they find it more and more difficult to manage. Finally the lions abandon the kill after one of them breaks a tooth in a vain effort to open new parts of the frozen hide.

Soon the snow is tracked with footprints leading to the bison's carcass. Wolves and smaller carnivores gnaw the bones. Ravens tease morsels from every surface they can reach, including the eyes, but the rest of the head and the legs remain untouched, folded under the body and protected by frozen hide. By late winter the bison is largely hidden under trampled snow.

Spring sunlight climbs higher and stronger until winter breaks in a rapid thaw. Snowmelt sheets down the slope, covering the carcass with a layer of cool silt even before the first flies of the year have a chance to emerge. Summer rains carry more silt downslope and the earthen shroud thickens. Cool temperatures and a silty cover protect the remains of the bison from blowflies and normal decay. The carcass refreezes by early October and hardly thaws the second summer.

In a few years the site is invisible, submerged under annual deposits of silt eroded from the slope above the creek. New plants flourish on the rich soil. Deposition continues to raise the level of the soil surface until, eventually, summer thaws no longer reach the carcass. Permafrost creeps up and over the scavenged steppe bison.

Decades pass. Then centuries, tens of centuries, hundreds of centuries . . . Time recontours the hills and valley as lines and wrinkles do a face: I know this person, but his face has changed. Yes, this is the place, but it is not the same. The lions are gone; forests of birch and spruce climb the hill now. Downstream the pulse of a generator supplies pressure to a jet of water like a massive fireman's hose. It cuts open frozen soils that clog the old valley floor. The water carves bizarre forms in the wall of frost and muck, washing away fossil cold and releasing a heavy organic odor. Silt particles flow away in the moving water, exposing the heavier gravel and gold. These are the sounds and smells of placer mining.

It was here, at a creek near Fairbanks, that Walter Roman found legs protruding from frozen silt in the muck canyon of his gold mining operation. Not just bones, these were real legs with hooves, hide and other tissues. Mr. Roman had found a frozen mummy! The hooves were those of a bison; blue crystals of vivianite were already forming on the exposed hide. Remembering Paul Bunyan's massive ox, we called the mummy Blue Babe.

Like a mysterious trunk from a deceased relative, or a skeleton found in the wall during renovations, Blue Babe is a strange inheritance. What is this: something to throw away or something to treasure?

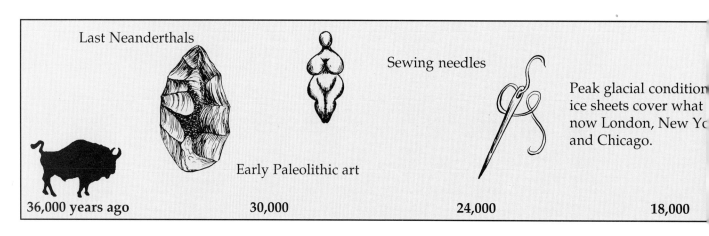

Last Neanderthals

Sewing needles

Early Paleolithic art

Peak glacial condition ice sheets cover what now London, New Yo and Chicago.

36,000 years ago   30,000   24,000   18,000

Bison priscus, *the splendid bison animating cave walls in Lascaux and Altimira, once grazed the rolling hills of interior Alaska. While nearly half of North America was covered by ice, central Alaska remained unglaciated. Wooly mammoth, steppe bison, ponies, camels, saiga antelope, lions and other animals thrived in regions characterized today by boreal forest and tundra.*

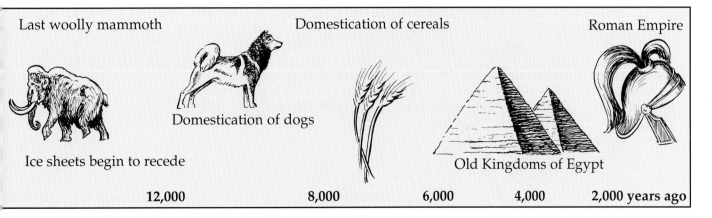

Last woolly mammoth

Domestication of cereals

Roman Empire

Domestication of dogs

Ice sheets begin to recede

Old Kingdoms of Egypt

| 12,000 | 8,000 | 6,000 | 4,000 | 2,000 years ago |

Pleistocene Alaska and the Mammoth Steppe

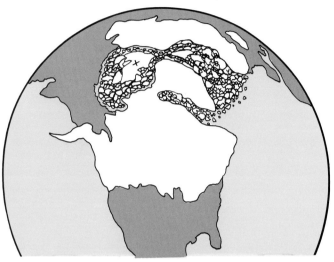

Asian Alaska: during the long glacial episodes, lower sea levels linked Alaska to Asia. At the same time, continental ice barred connections to the south. Alaskan plants and animals were virtually the same as those in much of northern Asia.

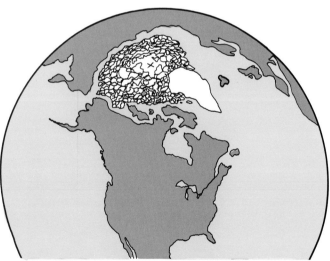

American Alaska: during warmer episodes, Alaska's overland connection to Asia was inundated. The warmer weather opened an ice-free corridor to the south, allowing animals and plants to enter and leave Alaska and the Yukon. Trees recolonized Alaska during these slightly wetter and warmer periods.

Long episodes of warm and cold have marked the past two million years of Earth's history. During cold periods, or glacials, accumulating snow in the coastal and Alaskan ranges formed vast ice fields. At times these ice fields actually coalesced with the expanding continental ice mass. So much moisture was held in ice that sea levels dropped 300 feet, exposing shallow continental shelf lands around the globe.

When glacial ice severed connections between Alaska and the south, these lowered sea levels opened a landbridge across the Bering Strait, linking unglaciated Alaska to Asia and Europe in a vast, largely treeless landscape named the Mammoth Steppe, after its largest inhabitant.

For tens of thousands of years the most numerous large mammals on the Mammoth Steppe were grazers: animals that eat grasses and other non-woody plants, quite unlike moose or deer, which thrive on woody winter browse. There were mixed feeders and some non-grazers on the scene as well. Museum panoramas of Pleistocene Alaska show a curious cast of characters. The diversity of large animal remains is striking. Furthermore, we know from the large body size and flamboyant horns and antlers that some species actually thrived at these high latitudes. Their trophy size suggests an environment with seasonally abundant food of top quality. And there were carnivores to match: lions, saber-tooth cats, wolves and two species of bears. Although animal densities were probably much lower than those of modern African savannas, the sheer presence of lions suggests there were more large mammals on the Mammoth Steppe than exist today in Alaska's tundra and boreal forest lands.

Plant and animal movements triggered by Pleistocene climatic changes are reflected in our present biota. Alaskan woodland species like spruce, porcupine and beavers are more similar to counterparts in Maine than Siberia because woodland biota reentered Alaska from the south during warmer periods. The heritage of our glacial landbridge connections to Asia include grizzlies, caribou, mountain sheep and lemmings.

(Right) Paleoclimatic indicators from deep cores of ocean sediments reflect the earth's changing climate. Blue Babe lived between the twin peaks of the last glacial.

There are thousands of glaciers in Alaska today. Ice fields as large as some states still cover parts of Alaska. Most of these occur in mountainous areas where the necessary ingredients of cold and moisture coincide. (Photo: Susan Karl)

A typical Alaskan scene: yet this moose and its surrounding vegetation are part of a new, Holocene Alaska, one that has developed only in the last 12,000 years.

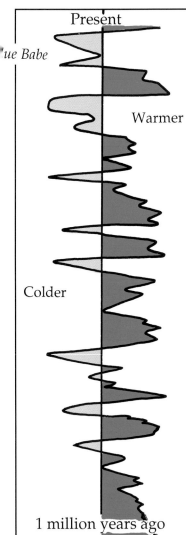

Present

ue Babe

Warmer

Colder

1 million years ago

4

Gold, Bones and Ivory

The grinding weight of glacial ice works like a mill, producing fine particles of rock flour that ride summer meltwater downstream to river bars and outwash plains. Air cooled by the ice mass flows down the glacier, creating winds that sort sand into dunes and send smaller silt and clay particles aloft. This dust can travel for miles. During the Pleistocene, fine layers of it fell year after year, accumulating the tan loess mantle visible in many interior Alaskan road cuts. Rain or snowmelt easily set the tiny silt particles in motion again. Bones, seeds, pollen, roots and occasionally soft body tissues were incorporated in valley deposits of reworked silt.

Innumerable remnants of the Pleistocene were buried this way. Winter frost and additional layers of silt combined to create the ultimate in cold storage. When this underground vault is opened at a construction site or by an eroding river bank, Pleistocene fossils commonly turn up. But the majority of items in museum collections from Pleistocene Alaska were found by men in pursuit, not of the past, but of gold.

Gold that eroded from exposed schist much earlier in the Pleistocene was carried downslope and buried in gravels just above bedrock, where it was slowly covered by layers of reworked silt and organic debris, often many yards deep and solidly frozen. Placer miners have used a variety of methods to reach the buried gravel and hoped-for gold. First they must strip away the insulating cover of vegetation so that the frozen silt can thaw. Jets of water have traditionally been used to speed defrosting and remove the silty muck. During the north's annual summer gold rush, ice wedges, layers of peat from warmer periods, fossil bones, teeth and, rarely, frozen mummies have been unearthed.

(Right) Pleistocene fossils in interior Alaska are most often found in deposits of reworked loess in valley bottoms. Here the skull of a woolly mammoth has been preserved in frozen silt. Ice wedges gleam in the background.

(Below) A placer miner strips away vegetation and frozen silt to reach gold bearing gravel below. Water is sprayed on the muck to speed thawing.

A road near Fairbanks cuts through deep deposits of windblown dust, called loess. Verticle loess cliffs, like these, are fairly stable, but loess is subject to rapid erosion when exposed in angled cuts of bare hillsides.

Discovery

idsummer, 1979, my husband Dale was asked to come see a mummified animal found at a placer gold mine near Fairbanks. Walter Roman, the mine operator, had collected many Pleistocene fossils over the years, but these were not bare bones. The cloven hooves and legs of an Ice Age bison were protruding from a wall of frozen muck!

Mr. Roman helped with the excavation, moving his water jets to other areas of the mine, allowing the wall of muck to thaw slowly. Over the next two weeks Dale collected sediments, mapped characteristics of the exposure and noted features of the landscape for clues about the bison's death and deposition. What would we find once frost freed the body? Was the mummy complete?

Thawing muck releases a musty reverberant smell, heavy with the life that once flowed in the plants and animals kept for millenia from their path to dust. Our work in the cold shadow of the mine exposure was grave and gay at once, and very, very muddy.

Perhaps this bison died at the hands of hunters? Maybe some of the first people to enter the New World? We found red flesh when we scraped into still frozen parts of the carcass. Dale's estimate of age (35,000 years) based on the bison's position in the layered silt and peat deposits was at once astounding and believable. The unimaginably old and the living were joined as the bison's decay, for so long halted, again rushed toward completion.

The legs and torso of the bison, as well as bags of silt, detached bones and hair were taken to the Fairbanks campus and refrozen. We still were waiting for the head — if indeed it was there at all — to emerge from the frozen silt. Finally a horntip showed. The head was there! In several days the bank thawed enough to remove the entire head, and at this point Mr. Roman allowed newsmen into the mine to photograph and publicize the find. Eyes closed, blue with vivianite, Blue Babe met the 20th Century.

Dale Guthrie excavating Blue Babe. Buckets of silt are being removed from the site for wet screening in the laboratory.

Blue Babe as he appeared at Walter Roman's mine.

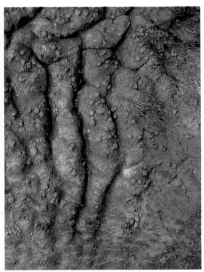

Close-up view of Blue Babe's skin. Vivianite is an iron phosphate that turns blue when oxidized. It occurs when organic remains low in iron and high in phosphates are buried in damp silt that is rich in iron but phosphate poor.

Walter Roman stands with his giant monitor at the mine where he found Blue Babe.

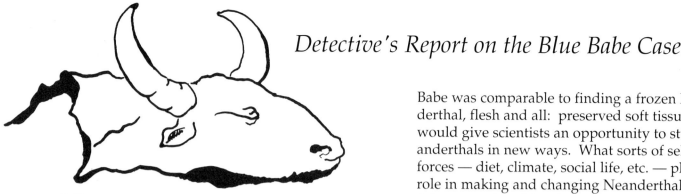

Detective's Report on the Blue Babe Case

Blue Babe had been found. What was the next step? Other Pleistocene mummies have been thoroughly washed down and made public as leathery curiosities. It was tempting to do the same with Blue Babe, but the carcass would only deteriorate further if it thawed and dried. Preserving evidence was paramount. After the photo session, Dale wrapped Blue Babe's head in damp cloth and plastic to prevent dehydration and packed it with the torso in a university freezer.

If Dale had written to Holmes and Watson at this point, his report might have read: "Mature male steppe bison found. Eight or nine years of age, apparently died in the winter from unknown causes. The body was scavenged before being buried and preserved in cold silt for thirty to forty thousand years."

Horns and male genitalia showed this was a male. The age was estimated from horn annulae, constrictions made when horns stop growing each winter. Dale thought it was possible the bison had died simply from winter debilitation. Winter underfur was present and many animals do succumb to stresses that accumulate in long northern winters. Even without cleaning, it was obvious that the carcass had been scavenged after death and before burial; vertebrae were missing, skin was torn, and most muscle masses were absent, while muscle tissues that remained were fairly well preserved.

To the imaginative detective, evidence is as much a matter of collecting questions as finding answers. Even Sherlock Holmes could not recognize some answers until he framed them in the appropriate questions. Before Blue Babe was cleaned and thawed, Dale wanted to have his pockets full of plans.

What did he hope to learn from this mummy? Skeletons of steppe bison abound; why was Blue Babe so important? Dale explained it this way: we know from fossil remains that bison evolved very rapidly, undergoing remarkable changes in a fairly short time, rather like people. In fact, finding Blue Babe was comparable to finding a frozen Neanderthal, flesh and all: preserved soft tissues would give scientists an opportunity to study Neanderthals in new ways. What sorts of selective forces — diet, climate, social life, etc. — played a role in making and changing Neanderthals, or in this case, steppe bison?

Blue Babe provided a chance to take a careful look at a steppe bison: bone structure, tooth wear, even plant fragments contained in tiny pockets in the teeth could be analyzed; gut contents and other parts of the carcass awaited study. Dale was particularly eager to reconstruct Blue Babe's outer appearance, the color and pattern of his hair, the size of his hump, and so on.

Bodies carry history and respond to life in different ways. Some features are much more plastic, more likely to change than others. For example, skull and horns can change remarkably. Feet and teeth on the other hand are usually very conservative, tied as they are to diet, digestion, and mobility.

Although most of us don't think of it this way, much social behavior actually has genetic structure. Tigers are solitary; they not only lack the complex social behavior of lions, but individual tigers cannot be trained into more sociable ways. In living animals we can study social behavior, but when it comes to extinct species, Dale and other paleobiologists must use whatever they can find to help them with the puzzle of the past. Teeth and bones are obvious tools, but soft tissues, the social organs animals "wear" — hair color and patterning, humps and wattles or the size and shape of penis tufts — can help explain social organization and behavior.

In the spring semester before the bison mummy was found, Dale was awarded sabbatical leave for a year of research in Europe and the Soviet Union. Our sabbatical plans changed after Blue Babe appeared, but we were headed in the right direction. Dale could discuss post-mortem procedures and mounting and display problems with Soviet colleagues who had worked on Siberian Pleistocene mummies. He wanted to study European collections of late Pleistocene fossils as well as actual representations of steppe bison in Paleolithic art.

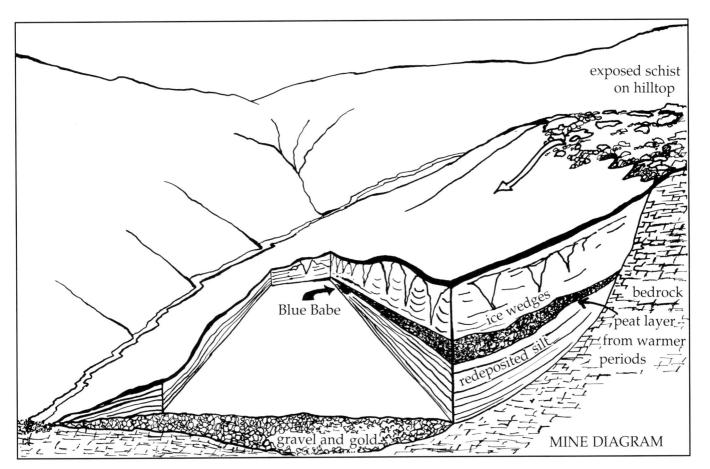

exposed schist on hilltop

Blue Babe

ice wedges

redeposited silt

bedrock

peat layer from warmer periods

gravel and gold.

MINE DIAGRAM

Also, Dale wanted to see a species of European bison that lives in reserves in the U.S.S.R., in Poland and in various zoos. These bison, known as wisent, are possibly Blue Babe's closest living relatives. Indeed, the whole issue of the relationship of American plains bison, European wisent and the Pleistocene steppe bison was something Dale hoped the mummy might clarify. Just weeks after Blue Babe was secured in a freezer with double temperature alarms, we flew to Europe.

Alaska

• Fairbanks

Blue Babe was found near Fairbanks, Alaska

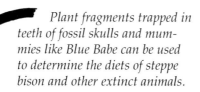

Plant fragments trapped in teeth of fossil skulls and mummies like Blue Babe can be used to determine the diets of steppe bison and other extinct animals.

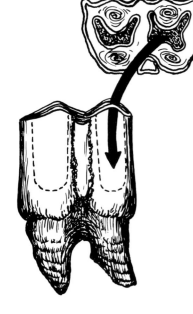

The radiocarbon date of a piece of Blue Babe's skin provided a more precise time of death: 36,000 years ago. A twig taken from a peat layer about a yard above the bison dated 30,000 years old, supporting the reliability of the first date.

Paleolithic Art

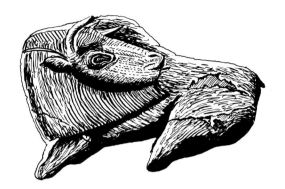

During sabbatical we visited zoos, museums and caves. We looked for remnant populations of European bison in Polish forests and saw, in the dim corner of a museum under semipermanent restoration, a woolly rhinocerous mummy awaiting its second resurrection. In Leningrad we lunched on boar knuckles with another hunter-paleontologist while discussing the mammoth mummies downstairs. To map patterns of skin thickness, we stuck straight pins into a fading wisent hide stored in a German palace.

Studying old bones is slightly old fashioned, comfortably out of style. Its popularity peaked in Edwardian times when the Ice Age was a new discovery and exploration of the globe and cataloging of the earth's living and recently living creatures was of keen interest. Indeed some places we visited looked as if they too had been in cold storage for 50 years. Late Pleistocene relics are not highlighted on many 21-day European tours.

There is one famous exception: the cave paintings of southwestern France and northern Spain. Steppe bison, woolly mammoths and rhinoceros, horses and asses, aurochs, caribou, lions and bears are drawn, painted and cut into cave walls.

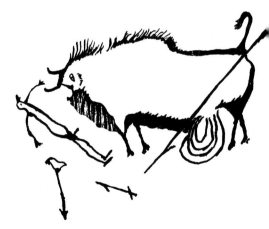

This famous Paleolithic drawing of a hunter and injured bison is one of a very few that show a person and animal together.

Lascaux and a number of less famous caves and sites containing Paleolithic art have been found near the Vezere River. Today the Vezere winds through a particularly lovely part of rural France; 15,000 years ago it was home to woolly mammoth, saiga antelope, caribou and bison like Blue Babe.

Sculpted and incised figures also occur in the region, including two bison modeled in clay that were preserved inside a cave. Paleolithic art has been found elsewhere in Europe, but this one area is extraordinarily rich.

These paintings and sculptures were made between 10,000 and 30,000 years ago by people hunting mammoths and other large mammals in a landscape that is now small valley farms and wooded hills. Europe has changed since the Pleistocene! Meeting these randomly preserved images I felt less distance than kinship and discovery. Here were real animals: the seen, the heard, hunted and eaten, feared and honored, defecating, grazing, mating, fighting, everyday animals of the Mammoth Steppe. Some I knew from home: caribou, muskoxen and bears were familiar; other species I'd met as teeth and skulls in museum cabinets, varnished bones with accession numbers in India ink. Paleontologists are at home with skeletons of extinct species, but Paleolithic art is altogether different. For anyone who will look, it holds the memories of living animals.

Hundreds of Paleolithic images of steppe bison exist, so although there is no photograph, we have many portraits which can be studied to see the bison they represent. Dale used these late Pleistocene steppe bison portraits in his investigation along with traditional paleontological evidence, studies of other mummies and work with living European and American bison.

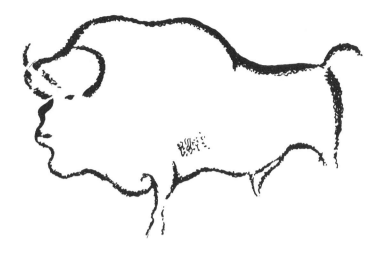

Most of these Paleolithic portraits are of male bison. A beard starts just behind his mouth and goes down the brisket to the forelegs. He has a hump that extends more than halfway along his back and horns that sweep up with a slight forward tilt.

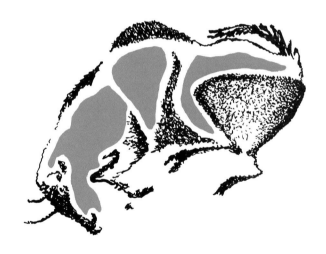

Colored pictures show a reddish brown body with darker legs, face, mane and tail. These cave art bison lack the hairy bonnets and pantaloons of American plains bison.

Common Animals of the Mammoth Steppe

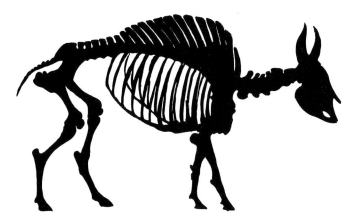

Steppe bison
(Bison priscus)

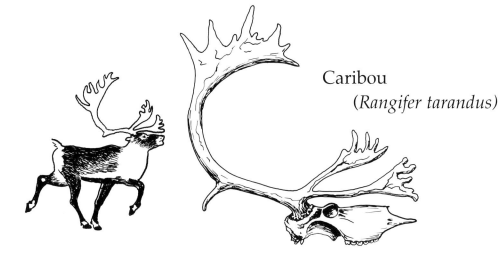

Caribou
(Rangifer tarandus)

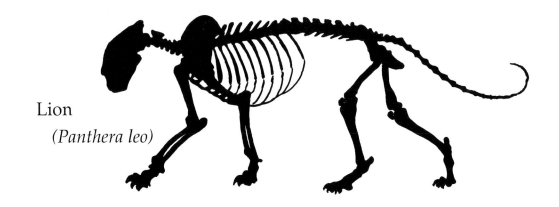

Lion
(Panthera leo)

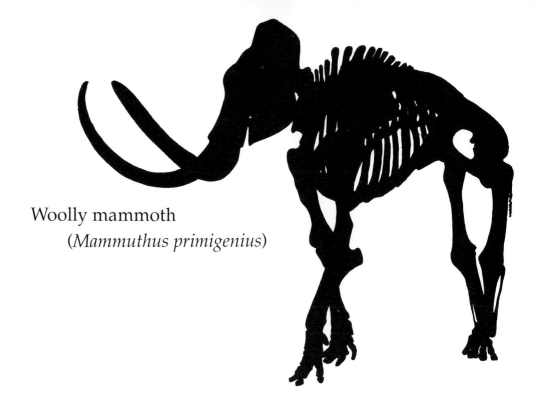

Woolly mammoth
(*Mammuthus primigenius*)

Pleistocene horse
(*Equus ferus*)

Saiga antelope
(Saiga tatarica)

Wolf
(*Canis lupus*)

Muskox
(*Ovibos moschatus*)

14

Steppe Bison Family History

Leptobos

Bison priscus

Bison latifrons

Bison antiquus

Bison bison

Blue Babe and other steppe bison were the descendants of a smaller-bodied, smaller-horned, ancestor named *Leptobos*. Bison evolved rapidly from this cattle-like ancestor, expanding their range into the north and entering the New World via the exposed land bridge, about 300,000 years ago.

From Alaska, some of these early New World bison moved south, where they evolved into giants. Fossil skulls have been found of these *Bison latifrons,* with horn cores over two yards wide. Bison ranged from California to Florida, but they were concentrated just east of the Rocky Mountains, from Alberta to Texas.

Bison latifrons graded into a smaller (though still quite large) form, called *Bison antiquus,* during the last glacial episode, 10,000 to 30,000 years ago. Bison in the Old World also became slightly smaller during this time.

As the ice began receding about 12,000 years ago at the beginning of the most recent period — the Holocene — there were dramatic changes in the vast band of habitat that had so long been home to bison. Formerly huge ranges were split into smaller segments, interrupted by woody vegetation unsuitable for bison. Bison populations became isolated and, again, the average body size diminished. As more of their open range became wooded, bison were edged out of some areas altogether; they became locally extinct over much of their former territory.

Pleistocene horses, saiga antelope, musk oxen, and other species experienced similar reductions and displacements but they were all able to find habitats where conditions allowed them to survive. Woolly mammoths also diminished in size and distribution, but for mammoths, the local extinctions kept accumulating to the point of complete species extinction, perhaps in some instances assisted by humans.

The Holocene changes that caused such disruption for many Pleistocene species also created new habitats that happened to suit the capabilities of other species. Moose, for example, were a minor species during the Pleistocene, but today moose are abundant in northern forests around the world, from Norway to Maine.

Today there are two species of bison: *Bison bonasus* or European wisent, and *Bison bison*, the American plains bison. Although the skeletons of wisent and American bison are very similar, the living animals are easily distinguished. There are striking differences in hair length and color. If we had only their skeletons, we might think wisent and plains bison were almost identical. In the absence of living steppe bison, the Blue Babe mummy allows us to learn more about the overall appearance of Alaskan steppe bison and thus, its relationship to other bison.

Wisent seem to have responded to the spreading forests of Holocene Europe by an evolutionary regression towards woodland-edge adaptations

The bison of the American plains, Bison bison.

The European wisent, Bison bonasus.

similar to those of wild cattle. Wisent even mark their territory like wild cattle. Male wisent don't clash heads to determine dominance and breeding rights but push head-to-head instead. Wisent once lived in England and Europe, but nowhere did they approach the great numbers of American plains bison. Since they lived in smaller populations, individual wisent could be acquainted with their neighbors. This difference in social life is reflected in the less gaudy social ornamentation of wisent in contrast to American bison. Wisent had become rare by the 16th century and now there are only a few herds living in special reserves.

Pleistocene Bison Belt. During the later half of the Pleistocene, bison were widely distributed across arid northern regions and continual genetic exchange kept bison rather closely related. Bison populations at the ends of the belt, in western Europe and on the American plains, were the most different.

The Post Mortem, 36,000 Years After Death

Necropsy work on the bison involved a careful look at every part of the mummy for clues about its life and death. (Photo: Institute of Arctic Biology)

Dale started necropsy work on Blue Babe the spring after we returned from sabbatical leave in Europe. First he thawed and screened bags of silt that had been collected during the excavation. Insect carcasses that were found were sent to appropriate specialists and silt samples were submitted to other labs for pollen analysis.

Next, the mummy's torso and legs were brought into the lab. Again, silt cleaned from the carcass was wet-screened. As the carcass was cleared of mud, the extent of scavenging became more apparent. Most of the hide was present, but it had been torn open down the back. Only the legs, neck and head were intact. Meat on the hams, back and shoulders was gone and many vertebrae were missing, but the sternum and lower ribs were present. Perhaps this animal had simply died peacefully, with its legs tucked underneath, protected from the chewing and pecking of scavengers?

As work progressed, Dale was surprised to find a substantial amount of fat in the bison. This didn't fit his image of a debilitated animal succumbing to the rigors of winter. Thick subcutaneous fat is not characteristic of northern ungulates in late winter, especially not one dead from internal causes. Had Blue Babe been killed by a predator?

A second surprise was the discovery of long scratch marks on the rear of the hide cutting deeply into the dermis. The scratches occurred in clusters of three and four parallel lines, like those made by the claws of a large predator. Wolves do not use their claws to kill prey. Grizzlies have powerful claws, but they do not retract like a cat's and thus are not sharp enough to repeatedly incise a thick hide. Modern day grizzly bears use their blunted claws primarily for digging out ground squirrels.

Dale puzzled over the scratch marks for several days before the realization struck: the scratches on Blue Babe's flanks were made by lions! Lions were in Alaska during the Pleistocene. Dale checked the literature on African lions and found descriptions of similar claw marks on African buffalo that had survived lion attacks. There were also accounts of African lions working together to kill mature bull buffalo; again, claw wounds were observed on the rear of the buffalo.

Returning to Blue Babe's hide for a closer look, Dale found pairs of round punctures, three-and-a-half inches apart. The spacing of these punctures matched exactly with the incisors of an Alaskan Pleistocene lion skull in the museum collections.

When the bison's heavy facial skin was pried back, clotted blood and additional punctures were revealed on the snout. Lions kill smaller animals, like gazelles or saiga antelope, with a neck bite that traumatizes the central nervous cord. Zebra, wildebeest, buffalo and other large prey require a different approach. First, lions must pull the prey down. Death is actually caused by strangulation when the lion encloses the snout of its victim in an airtight bite.

Alaskan lions, lions hunting in the hills near our home, had taken this bison. We saw Blue Babe in a different light. The image of lions stalking, attacking a large steppe bison fore and aft, was more dynamic and probably more true to the way things once were here.

This new twist gave life to Dale's reconstruction work with Blue Babe, like a faded photograph blossoming into color and motion, we now had a picture of lions hunting Blue Babe; lions living here in the far north; lions in action.

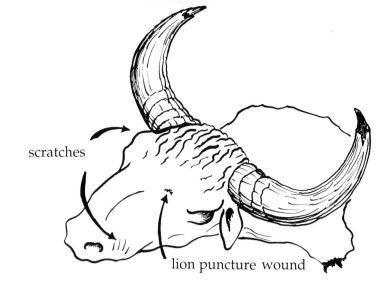

Wounds on Blue Babe's head

Clotted blood found under the skin

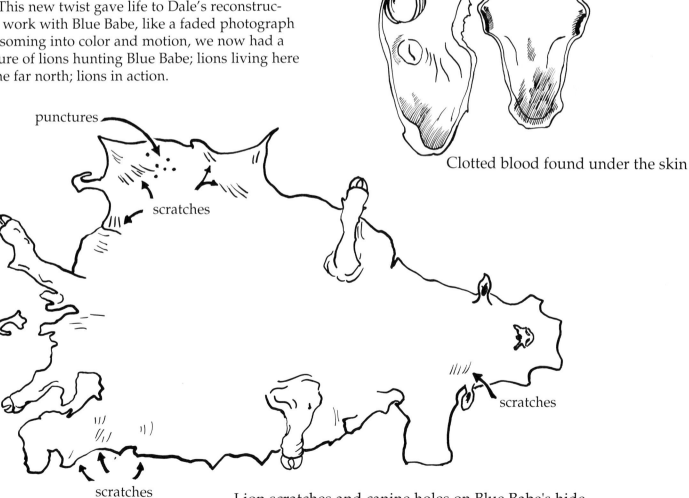

Lion scratches and canine holes on Blue Babe's hide.

Alaskan Lions

Although lion remains are uncommon compared to the vast numbers of mammoth, horse and bison fossils, there are some Pleistocene Alaskan lion skulls in museum collections. Alaskan Pleistocene lions were the same size as modern African lions and probably were similar in general behavior as well.

It may be difficult to imagine lions prowling the cold expanses of the Mammoth Steppe, but lions, like many other large mammals, actually can tolerate a broad range of temperatures without pulling out every metabolic stop or freezing to death. Our thermoneutral zone is only 20 or 30 degrees. We can manage life outside these rather precise temperatures only with extra clothing, fire and shelter. Moose, in contrast, apparently enjoy a thermoneutral range of more than 100 degrees, feeding placidly on willow twigs at -40. The mercury must drop to -60 before these long-legged deer increase their metabolic rate. Our intuitive understanding of lions must expand to include Pleistocene lions living year round near the Arctic Circle, hunting on catpaws adapted to below zero snows.

But cold is only one factor. Food and competition for food are usually more decisive limitations. How much food does a lion require? We know that lions were in Alaska and that they cannot hibernate as bears do. Lions are not known for thousand mile migrations; apparently enough prey was available during the long winters for generations of lions to survive. Furthermore, other large predators, competing with lions, also occupied the Mammoth Steppe. Could lions live in Alaska today? Probably not. There is simply not enough to eat within reach, especially in the vast interior of the state. Once again Dale turned to Paleolithic art, this time to search for images of lions and other predators.

Compared to the images of Pleistocene bison, horses, mammoth or caribou, there are only a handful of lion pictures from the Paleolithic. These lions have little or no shaggy mane, and usually only one or two lions are shown together.

Dale found these characters significant. Today, not all male lions have large, showy neck manes. Manes are most luxurious in areas where male lions are the head of large prides of females who do nearly all the hunting. At the other extreme, in marginal desert habitats where prey is scarce, male lions do not develop large manes at all. These

Mature male lion living in the Kalahari. His lightly colored mane is of modest size. Male Alaskan lions probably had even smaller manes.

males hunt for their own food along with the females and the lions do not live in large prides. Conditions for many lions fall between these extremes; the male lion develops a modest mane that allows him to hunt with the females in his pride. The most flamboyant manes, of course, often attract the attention of prey as well as other lions. These largest manes handicap the wearer when it comes to hunting.

The fact that the cave art lions had skimpy manes and that they were usually shown singly, or in pairs, suggested to Dale that Pleistocene lions had a social organization similar to that of African lions living under difficult conditions; that is, the Alaskan lions probably lived and hunted singly, or in pairs, and the males had very limited manes.

Later, when Blue Babe's hide was being split for tanning and museum display, Eirik Granqvist, the preparator, found a chip of tooth in the hide. This tooth chip was small, but thick enamel and contours of the fragment allowed Dale to identify it as part of a lion carnassial. It also added to our picture of Blue Babe's death.

Dale used George Schaller's studies of African lions to determine how much of the bison carcass the Pleistocene lions could have consumed before the remaining flesh froze stone hard. Two or three lions, gorging on 30 pounds of meat a day, would still have been unable to eat all the bison in less than four days. And in that time, at winter temperatures, an opened carcass would be frozen. Judging from the broken lion's tooth, at least one lion was still on the scene, trying to eat more, after the carcass had frozen. Of course the legs and other parts of the body still encased in skin would have been the most difficult to reach once the body froze.

Did a single lion kill Blue Babe? Probably not. Mature bull buffalo are common, though far from easy, targets of attack by African lions. The solitary life of the ornery bulls makes them more susceptible to lion attacks than the cows and calves living in herds, but lone bulls are rarely killed by single lions. Usually it is two or three lions hunting together that have the most success bringing down large bull buffalo. Since Blue Babe had formidable defenses in his horns — as long as he could stay on his feet — he could probably have kept head-to-head with a single lion and fended off an attack.

African buffalo. Present day interactions between African lions and buffalo are roughly analogous to Alaskan Pleistocene lions and steppe bison like Blue Babe.

Dale's reconstruction of an Ice Age Alaskan lion.

The post mortem did solve the mystery of what killed Blue Babe, but other questions remained. It's easy to imagine a lion returning to the bison carcass, tugging unsuccessfully at the frozen hide, hungry enough to break a tooth in its effort. What happened next?

There is evidence that smaller mammalian scavengers and birds used the bison carcass. During his years in Alaska, Dale has seen similar signs of scavenging by ravens and small mammals on numerous moose and caribou winter kills. Also, Gary Haynes' work in Wood Buffalo Park in northern Alberta provided very useful parallels.

Gary Haynes is an archeologist interested in taphonomic processes. He traveled to the park one winter to observe the death and events that follow the death of bison. Wolves are the main predators in the park and Haynes watched the action around a number of bison carcasses throughout the winter. His work showed that bison did sometimes die with their legs folded underneath — as it seemed Blue Babe had — and it supplied vivid assurance that a picture of Blue Babe killed in late fall or early winter, partly eaten and the frozen remains scavenged until spring, was plausible. The part of the story that remained cloudy in Dale's mind had to do with the how and when of the bison's burial. Of course, the challenge in making a frozen mummy lies in burial. It has to occur rapidly, before the body is eaten up or decomposed. Plenty of theories had been proposed for other frozen mummies: a fall into a thermokarst pit, instant burial when an overhanging bank collapsed, drowning in cold mud, and so on. The careful excavation that was possible with Blue Babe meant more evidence than usual was available about his burial, and it simply didn't support these theories.

Just for an experiment, Dale brought home a dead bison. When he read in the paper that several bison had died from drinking snowmelt water at a fertilizer spill near Delta, about 100 miles from Fairbanks, he borrowed a truck and got permission from the local Fish and Game office to haul one of the bison home. It was below zero and snow fell the next few days, but something peculiar was going on, the bison wasn't covered with snow.

Inside the unopened carcass and insulating pelt, the bison's gut was as hot as a very successful compost pile. Dale opened the belly and pulled the steaming contents out into the snow. There was another month of hard cold. The carcass was popular with ravens and the neighbors' dogs, but things really picked up after breakup.

Flies found the carcass. Within a few weeks they reduced the bison to bone, hair and fly pupae cases. It happened so fast the first green grass of spring grew in among bare bones, raising a new issue about Blue Babe's burial. Fly pupae cases hadn't been found with the mummy.

Blowfly and scavenger beetle remains commonly occur with Alaskan Pleistocene fossils, but they weren't found during the post mortem even though fifty pounds of red muscle remained on the carcass. This flesh would have been protected from scavenging by frozen leg, neck and head skin during the winter following death, but surely it was a prime target once exposed by spring thaw. Blue Babe must have been buried soon after breakup.

Dale sorted through his records from the excavation and returned to the mine to study the valley again. The carcass had been found in a thick bed of silt with many layers of thinly bedded silt above. It was positioned downslope of a large hill and slightly to the side of the old valley stream bed.

A cold, if not still frozen carcass, lying on frozen soils and buried under a bed of cold silt, would decay little in the short summer. Subsequent washing and deposits of silt would raise the ground surface, eventually pulling the zone of permafrost upward until the bison was incorporated in a silty deep freeze.

But how could such rapid deposit of silt occur? The slope wasn't steep enough for mudslides. Dale felt the key factor was vegetative cover. Even today, in construction sites and roadsides where loess is not protected by vegetation, a sudden inch of rain can erode deep gullies. With more open soil surfaces typical of the Mammoth Steppe, just sheet-washed silt carried by snowmelt or early rains could have buried the bison. No doubt it was unusual for silt to bury a carcass like Blue Babe, but in geologic time, hardly ever is often enough.

As soon as spring temperatures allowed, flies reduced this Alaskan bison carcass to bones within days.

Avian scavengers frequently leave evidence of their work on large mammal carcasses. Such characteristic stringy, tendonous fibers are visible here.

The scavenged carcass of this bison, killed by wolves in northern Alberta, illustrates the way Blue Babe may have appeared before he was buried. (Photo: Gary Haynes)

The spring after Blue Babe died, cold, silt-laden water flowed downslope, covering the carcass. The wet silt above and frozen ground below kept the body cool and limited decomposition.

Taphonomy

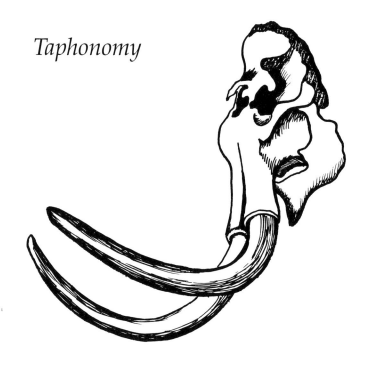

Taphonomy is a special branch of paleontology, concerned with the way in which organisms are preserved as fossils. Of course most organisms are not preserved: scavenging, decomposition, weathering and other natural processes return virtually all plants and animals to elemental parts. Recycling is the norm in nature.

Curiously, a frozen mummy requires both water and earth. You cannot make a mummy in the wintertime; it may feel quite possible during a January cold snap, but there is a difference between a frozen carcass and a mummy. Cartoons of woolly mammoths in a block of clear ice are only cartoons. Frozen mummies found in the unglaciated north were buried in earth, not sparkling ice. There is no evidence that these animals fell into glacial crevasses or were overtaken by huge snow drifts that later gellified. Siberian and Alaskan mummies were buried in earth and then kept cold. These same processes preserved a multitude of Pleistocene skulls, tusks and other bones: interment and cold. Except for hibernating ground squirrels and other animals likely to die underground, preservation of most northern fossil bones and mummies could begin only after spring thaw.

Thick valley deposits of reworked silt, like those at Pearl Creek that held Blue Babe, are a mixture of thin, finely bedded silt layers and occasional single-event beds of larger size. More exposed soil and heavier rains or spring snowmelt were required to transport these silts downslope.

Russian paleontologists have proposed that most late Pleistocene frozen mummies come from two periods: around 11,000 and 35,000 years ago. These may have been times when conditions for preservation were optimal: exposed soil on one hand and moisture on the other. During full glacial conditions, the amount of water, whether rainfall or snowmelt, was probably too meager to create sheet erosion. Such erosion would have been limited as well during the warmer, wetter interglacials, because these very conditions of additional warmth and moisture allowed more complete vegetative cover.

Today there is little widescale erosion and sheet-washing of silt because nearly all the soil surface is covered by plants and plant litter. Also, interior Alaska seldom receives heavy, violent rains. Most of our meager rainfall comes in small droplet showers. Chances for preservation of bones or soft tissue are negligible under present conditions.

No part of this dead African elephant will become a fossil. Burial is usually the first step toward fossilization. Animals which happen to die in depositional environments stand the best chance of being preserved.

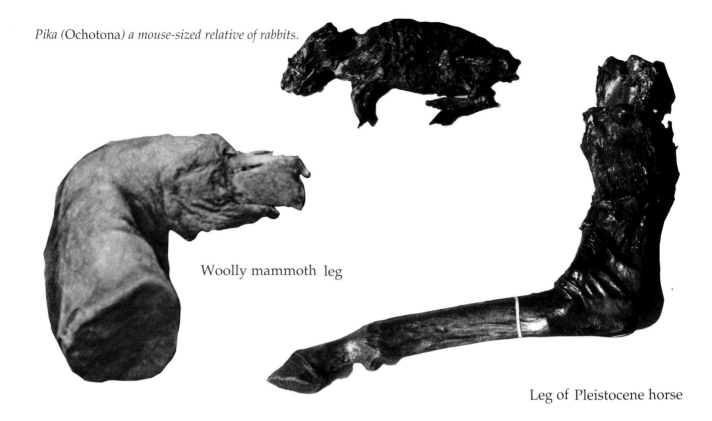

Pika (Ochotona) a mouse-sized relative of rabbits.

Woolly mammoth leg

Leg of Pleistocene horse

Mummified parts of other large animals have been found in Alaska. Hooves and lower legs are most numerous. Limbs cool rapidly after death and are thus less subject to decomposition. Also, the bony limbs covered with thick hide are less tempting to carnivores and scavengers than other parts.

Dima, a young Siberian mammoth, was also discovered by a gold miner. Dima was studied in detail, mounted, and is now displayed in the Leningrad Museum of Natural History.

(Photo: USSR Academy of Sciences)

24

New World Bison and Man

Excavation of the Dry Creek Camp Site near Healy, Alaska. This site on the northern edge of the Alaska Range dates back about 11,000 years ago.

Blue Babe was buried. As more silt washed down from the slope and settled above him, the thin warmth of summer could no longer touch the carcass or restore all of the heat pulled from the ground each winter. Frost, an almost permanent frost, held the bison for 36,000 years.

This is a long time. Our imagination labors to traverse 1000 years. To go back to Blue Babe and the lions, it must search for solid footing on points it has learned before: the Norman invasion, Caesar's Rome, early Egyptian dynasties, cultivation of grains, domestication of dogs, needles and sewn clothing, the Lascaux paintings, woolly mammoths and rhinos on the banks of the Thames. . . And the further back we go, the more the slope steepens toward the dark shaft of geologic time.

Blue Babe rests underground. Lions hunt at dusk. Bands of woolly mammoth cross the valley and horses and bison graze the slope above, relishing the new grass of early summer. The summer sun rolls around the horizon; winter sun hovers at the open edge of sky; marking the seasons, year after year.

Blue Babe lived during a milder, interstadial period that continued for more than 10,000 years after his death. About 25,000 years ago, climatic conditions gradually returned to full glacial. Slightly harder cold and perhaps drier weather made it impossible for trees to survive in the far north. Again, water borrowed from the seas accumulated in masses of glacial ice, closing connections to the south and turning the shallow Bering shelf lands into a vast plain. Yet, as in earlier full glacials, many large mammals continued to live in Alaska. These glacial conditions peaked around 18,000 years ago.

Then, around 12,000 years ago, as the steppe gave way to birch, poplar and other trees, and as mammoth, bison and horses were finding less and less they could eat, something altogether new happened. Warm specks of light shone in the winter landscape. People came into the country. Those first fires multiplied and spread; crossing a hemisphere with the flickering light of campfires, hearthfires, homefires. And every night, fires glowed across a continent that had known only intermittent wild fire.

They were hunters, these new ones, and they killed with a projectile: a point hafted to the end of a shaft that was cast through the air. There was no engaging of horns and claws, hooves and teeth. A few campsites of these earliest hunters have been excavated. Bones of sheep and elk and bison, dating around 11, 000 years old, were found at the Dry Creek site, along with the stone tools these people made and used.

Although there is some debate about the time people first entered the New World, there are archaeological sites throughout the continent that date from 11,500 to 11,000 years ago. Stone tools found at these sites show similarities in style, and there is no question that human populations were part of Holocene America at this time. Dating of glacial moraines left by retreating ice in the Canadian west indicates that movement through this area was indeed possible 12,000 years ago.

The story of bison in Holocene Alaska is rather fuzzy, partly because conditions for preservation of fossils are much more limited in the warmer, wetter climate of this period. Bison fossils do trickle down through the Holocene until about 500 years ago, yet there were no bison here when the first Europeans visited Alaska, and Native Alaskans had apparently lost the memory of bison in their words and stories.

Head-Smashed-In *buffalo jump in southwestern Alberta. Bison were an important resource for Indians in the American west. At this site and at many others, Indians were able to conduct mass kills. Some of these sites date to 11,000 years ago.*

American plains bison have been successfully introduced in Alaska. They are able to live in special habitats where winds from mountain passes produce grassy outwash flats and restrict snow cover. These are three young bulls near Delta, Alaska.

Mounting a Mummy

Since other Pleistocene mummies found in Alaska had not been mounted, sabbatical leave gave Dale a chance to see mounted mummies in European and Soviet museums and to talk with preparators about Blue Babe. Some Siberian mammoth mummies have been prepared much as a taxidermist would mount an elephant: a form of the mammoth was sculpted and cast into plaster and then the tanned skin was stretched over the plaster form. The resulting mammoth display is not a complete animal, somehow preserved entire, but a mannequin with tanned skin.

Fifty years ago, mounted animals in carefully painted dioramas were highlighted exhibits in most large natural history museums. Today, few museums even have taxidermy staff. Private taxidermists doing trophy work usually rely on pre-cast mannequins: one or two poses are made for each species, available in small, medium and large sizes. The time required to sculpt and cast original forms makes custom-made mannequins a luxury. As a result, sculptural skills involved in making anatomically accurate mannequins are rarely practiced.

Dale wondered where he would find the right taxidermist to handle Blue Babe; he discussed the problem with various people, among them Professor Bjorn Kurtén. Professor Kurtén is the author of numerous scientific works on Pleistocene subjects and has also written several novels set at the end of the Ice Ages. He introduced us to the conservator of the Helsinki Zoological Museum, Eirik Granqvist. We could see that Eirik was building an excellent large mammal exhibit at the museum with a minimal budget. Eirik found the prospect of mounting Blue Babe intriguing and corresponded with Dale about the project after we left Finland.

When the post-mortem work was finished, Eirik advised Dale to put Blue Babe's hide into vats of ethanol. The ethanol would preserve the hide until funds could be organized for Eirik to fly to Alaska and do the mounting. Meanwhile, Dale started to make a small sculpture of Blue Babe. He used anatomical information from the carcass, European Paleolithic art, fossil skeletons, and studies of living bison. Evening after evening, Dale fussed with the clay bison, reexamining his research in the clay form; how should this horn go, this hoof, the tail? When he was satisfied that further efforts were not improving the model, we made a mold of the clay bison. Using

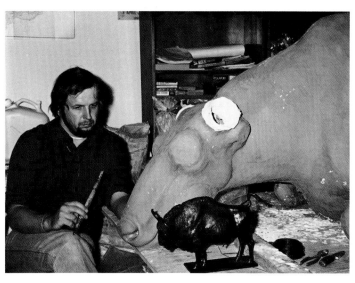

Eirik Granqvist models the original clay form of the mannequin, using Dale's bronze sculpture as a guide. (Photo: Institute of Arctic Biology)

the mold, we made a wax bison that was later cast in bronze at a foundry.

When Eirik arrived in Fairbanks in 1984, he and Dale used the bronze bison and Dale's drawings and photos to decide how to mount Blue Babe. They felt that reproducing the tangled carcass that appeared at Mr. Roman's mine was insufficient, but that a full standing mount would be too much. In the end they decided to position the mount as Blue Babe appeared when he died, lying down with legs gathered underneath the body.

Eirik set to work. Using the bronze model and measurements from Blue Babe and other steppe bison bones, Eirik made a plywood silhouette, adding limb bones for accurate leg dimensions. Next, he added chicken wire shaped to the wood, and on top of this rough shape he sculpted the body in plasticene clay. The head was developed separately. Eirik wrapped Blue Babe's skull in plastic film and modeled clay over the actual skull. When the head was modeled, Eirik made a mold and cast a copy in plaster. This plaster head was then attached to the body and refined with more clay and modeling.

Once the bison form was worked out in clay, Eirik was ready to make a piece mold in plaster. When complete and dry, this plaster piece mold was coated with releaser, the pieces assembled, and the final plaster form of the bison, reinforced with burlap, was cast in the mold.

Now, except for horns, the mannequin was ready. Dale wanted to keep Blue Babe's horns and head frozen for further studies, so he and Eirik made a mold of the real horns. After Blue Babe's own horns were returned to the freezer, this mold was used to cast epoxy horns for the museum display.

In addition to all the work making a mannequin, Eirik also had to clean and tan Blue Babe's hide. It was during this work that Eirik found the chip of lion's tooth embedded in the thick skin.

The skin was treated with chemicals to protect it from insects and decomposers, and with a relaxant. Then it was ready to pull over the plaster mannequin — almost a perfect fit. Eirik tacked the skin in place, then melted a wax mixture into the surface. Finally he installed the cast horns and touched up the skin surface with vivianite saved from the post-mortem. Once again blue, the bison was ceremoniously carried across the street to the museum.

Plywood silhouette

Modeling the clay original

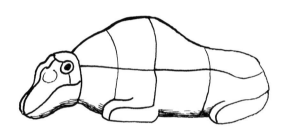

Making a plaster mold

Casting the mannequin in the plaster mold

Blue Babe's tanned skin is attached to the finished mannequin

A Taste of the Pleistocene

To celebrate Eirik's work and the new Blue Babe, we decided to cook a bison stew. A marvelous bit of luck had brought Bjorn Kurtén to Fairbanks for guest lectures and we invited other friends who were game enough to try the stew. Spring was underway. With a good burgundy to brace the rather muddy tone of the main dish, we toasted the past and present in the long evening twilight — a taste of the Pleistocene with friends who shared and had added to it with their talents and imagination. It was a special evening.

Now, so many years after Walter Roman first spotted Blue Babe, the mummy is part of a new museum display: his story finally ripe enough to tell. Although the old bison may still raise a question or two, the manuscript of Dale's book on Blue Babe shares space on my desk with this piece. Our enigmatic friend, discussed so often over breakfast tea, is about to move from the rooms of our lives into the peculiar habitat of print.

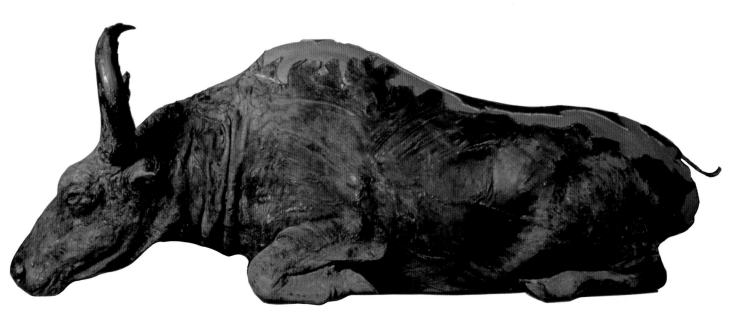

Blue Babe, mounted and on view at the University of Alaska Museum in Fairbanks. (Photo: University of Alaska Museum)

Tufts of it slip off the thawing hide,
soft and russet in my hand.
Bison priscus above miners gold
how old can we understand?

Scent of lion — nostrils flare —
you sight one; there was a pair.
At twilight I watch what no one saw:
hunger disregarding horns and hooves
pulls them to you, no easy kill.
Massive thrust, blurred motion
then not blood and gore
but simply lacking air, air....

She lets go your muzzle.
They tear and gorge,
groom and purr, sleep
satisfied while snow sifts
through your cooling hair.

Further Reading

For more on Blue Babe, see Dale Guthrie's book with the complete story. University of Chicago Press, 1989.

Buffalo Land, by William D. Berry, Macmillan, 1961.

Glaciers and Ice Age Alaska, by Dale and Mary Lee Guthrie, in *Alaska's Glaciers*, Alaska Geographic Vol. 9 /No. 1, 1982, pp. 34-43.

The Ice Age, by Bjorn Kurtén, G. Putnam's Sons, 1972.

Ice Ages: Solving the Mystery, J. Imbrie and K.P. Imbrie, Macmillan, 1979.

On the Track of Ice Age Mammals, Antony J. Sutcliffe, British Museum (Natural History), 1985.

Paleoecology of Beringia, D. Hopkins, J. Matthews, C. Schweger and S. Young, editors, Academic Press, 1982.

Pleistocene Rhymes and Seasonal Reasons, Dale and Mary Lee Guthrie, in *Interior Alaska: A Journey Through Time*, Alaska Geographic Society, 1986, pp. 53-95.

Quaternary Extinctions, Paul Martin and Richard Klein, editors, University of Arizona Press, 1984.

Acknowledgments

I would like to thank my family. Their encouragement and forbearance have been the best. Also, I want to note the generous help of Mary Calmes, Mary Medora Durbrow, Susan Morris Fabian, Jane Holding and Peggy Kuropat, my first readers.

Printing: Lorraine Press, Salt Lake City

ISBN   0-929324-01-3

Published by:
WHITE MAMMOTH
2183 Nottingham
Fairbanks, Alaska 99709

Mary Lee and Dale Guthrie

The Guthries live in Fairbanks, Alaska. Mary Lee is a writer and artist; Dale is a paleontologist and biology professor at the University of Alaska. As the local specialist on Ice Age fossils, Dale is often asked to look at bones and other interesting finds. But Walter Roman's discovery of a Pleistocene mummy in the permafrost of his gold mining operation was extraordinary. Dale and Mary Lee excavated the mummy, a steppe bison they named Blue Babe, which is now mounted and displayed at the University of Alaska Museum.

Ice Age mummies are uncommon. Blue Babe is the first North American frozen mummy to be excavated and studied in detail, and scientific work with the bison followed a number of surprising turns. This booklet was conceived during an early revision of Dale's much longer manuscript about Blue Babe. It is the nutshell version: from Mr. Roman's gold mine to the museum display, looking at Paleolithic art, lion skulls, death and detective work; a story about a steppe bison and time.